First published in Great Britain in 1980 by
Octopus Books Limited under the title
First Words

This edition published in 1988 by
Treasure Press
Michelin House
81 Fulham Road
London SW3 6RB

ISBN 1 85051 296 5

Printed by Mandarin Offset in Hong Kong

Educational and Series advisor Felicia Law

MY FIRST WORDS

Illustrated by
David Mostyn

TREASURE PRESS

The Attic

feather

skis

doll's house

telescope

doll

key

cobweb

spider

toboggan

hat

rocking horse

album

trunk

7

The Zoo

zebra

kangaroo

cheetah   chimpanzee

peacock

giraffe   penguin

camel

lion

tiger

alligator

bear

elephant

apron

freezer

cat

refrigerator

tap

sink

chair

cupboard

recipe

10

The Kitchen

tile

saucepan

cooker

mug

cup

iron

washing machine

ironing board

The Circus

tent

balloon

fire-eater

juggler

clown

trapeze

acrobat

pony

bucket

The Supermarket

sweets

till

counter

milk

sausage

meat

basket

The Park

pigeon

tree

greenhouse

orchard

dustbin

dog

picnic

pool

squirrel

acorn

ant

flower

16

kite

oak

apple

bonfire

wheelbarrow

pushchair

spade

rake

lawn-mower

swan

duck

rose

petal

The Marina

mast

hovercraft

jetty

sail

buoy

pontoon

sailor

yacht

dinghy

oar

rowing boat

rudder

cabin cruiser

deck

19

The Toyshop

jigsaw puzzle

teaset

cowboy

rag doll

parcel

pram

record player

puppet

frisbee

records

soldier

counter

skateboard

lifeguard

snorkel

swimsuit

foot

hair

armband

float

22

The Swimming Pool

window

tile

body

mouth

water

nose

hand

The Football Match

player

shorts

whistle

referee

goalpost

goalkeeper

camera

football

photographer

scarf

satellite

control tower

helmet

astronaut

26

Moon Base

moon

cone

planet

spaceship

rocket

launching pad

The Bedroom

curtains

mirror

picture

toy

pillow

carpet

slippers

blanket

lamp

dress

dressing gown

bed

socks

shoes

The Workshop

wire

torch

spring

ladder

paint

wood

pliers

ruler

saw

nails

hammer

drill

sawdust

31

railing

jeans

roundabout

slide

pocket

32

The Playground

puddle

umbrella

swings

climbing frame

seesaw

seagull

flag

sandals

bucket

deck-chair

sand-castle

crab

seaweed

34

The Beach

goggles

skin-diver

ferry

fisherman

pier

flippers

net

shell

pebble

blood

thermometer

patient

bandage

ointment

towel

The Hospital

doctor

ward

soap

nurse

37

The Pet Shop

bird

hutch

kitten

puppy

rabbit

sacks

38

birdcage

snake

guinea pig

mouse

39

The Restaurant

waitress

plate

glasses

lamp

knife

ice cream

spoon

fork

salad

mat

bowl

cola

tablecloth

chair

ABCDEFGHIJKL
MNOPQRSTUVW
XYZ abcdefghijklmn
opqrstuvwxyz

alphabet

ribbon

book

plasticine

table

The Classroom

teacher

pattern

scissors

paste

pencil

painting

paper

43

The Farmyard

combine harvester

shed

headlight

tractor

spade

wheel

hen

egg

field

gate

fence

farmer

pond

pig

straw